Our Held Animal
Breath

Our Held Animal Breath

Poems by Kathryn Kirkpatrick

WordTech Editions

Published by WordTech Editions
P.O. Box 541106
Cincinnati, OH 45254-1106

ISBN: 9781936370917
LCCN: 2012948546

Poetry Editor: Kevin Walzer
Business Editor: Lori Jareo

Visit us on the web at www.wordtechweb.com

Cover photo by Gary Bacon

Acknowledgements

My thanks to the editors, readers, and staff of the following journals where these poems first appeared, sometimes in other versions:

"Except This," *Another Chicago Magazine*; "Saying No to Thunder," *The Bark*; "To Have You Back," *Birmingham Poetry Review*; "1957" & "How to Lose a Democracy," *Blue Collar Review*; "Dog Dreams" & "Driving Home," *Cold Mountain Review*; "Millennium," "Recalling Virginia Woolf," & "Trackless," *Jelly Bucket*; "Canning Globalization" & ""News from Midlife," *Kakalak: An Anthology of Carolina Poets*; "At the Turkey Farm" & "Ars Poetica," *Pembroke Magazine*; "When the Hornets," "On Being Told Not to Use the Word Moral," "Mulch," "Before and After," & "Oblique," *Poem*; "Her Hatred," *Rattle*; "After Zazen" & "Removing Moles," *The Recorder*; "Kundalini," *Room of One's Own*; "The Floor," "Natal Chart," & "Touring the Czech Republic," *Southern Poetry Review*; "Stubbornly Green," *storySouth*; "Our Held Animal Breath," *The Southern Review*; "A Friend Visits the Sites of Vanished Civilizations," "Mysterious Friendship," "Well Before Danger," "Millennium ii," "The Zen Master Yells," & "Rescuing the Garden," *The South Carolina Review*; "Strange Meeting," *Terrain: A Journal of Built and Natural Environments*.

I am grateful to Applachian State for support in completing this manuscript, and to William Atkinson, Nathalie Anderson, Kathryn Stripling Byer, Susan Ludvingson, and Sharon Sharp for their careful attention to these poems.

In memory of

Karen Strickland, dear cousin
(1954-2006)

and

Barbara Mortimer, dear friend
(1960-2006)

Table of Contents

Millennium

A tethered fox
snarls and backs away.
I swim across a lake
to reach a thatched cottage.
Inside, a sudden staircase,
a carpet, worn, beyond price.
When I sit down at a desk,
cigarette butts at my left hand,
smoky slice of agate at my right,
I am alone with the rest of my life.
A man standing behind me
has mastered the art of change.
After he vanishes, I pull
down each heavy drape
and the rooms flood with light.
How did I come by this altar,
these windows of stained glass?
When I meet the fox again,
I set her free.
The meadow she finds
is neither desert nor glacier.

1

Before I woke I heard a woman's voice cry out.
It was hoarse with doubt.
She was saying,
I was saying—

What have we done?

Eavan Boland

A Friend Visits the Sites of Vanished Civilizations

She tells me the Anasazi ascended,
dropped the husks of their bodily selves
and returned to pure energy.

I speculate climate change,
food gone scarce, but she'll have
none of it.
　　　　　They were shape-shifters,
sometimes running on their four legs,
sometimes unfolding their wings.
Why not become the breath
rather than the animal breathing?

And it makes as much sense
as anything else
here at the surreal beginning
of the twenty-first century.
Aren't we all in the grips
of something more or less unbelievable?
Somnambulant citizens in a failing craft,
we watch the waters rise.

In the face of it
who among us would not wish to leave
altogether, not through the squalor
of disease or cracked bones,
but sudden and clean,
an indigenous rapture?

Here's what the Hopi say:

a serpent with plumes
brought a great flood, water
scouring red rock, uprooting
cottonwood and willows,
rising above the sandstone walls
of the city.
          The leaders
had stopped talking to the spirits
of the land, and the people,
the people let them.

Questions for a New Century

The common squirrel knows which acorn sprouts
quickly. Is it the red oak or white? She knows
and buries the one that will keep until
winter.
　　　When the acorn that keeps is scarce—
is it the red oak or white?—she knows how to nip
the germinating tip so that the other saves too
(the white oak, I think).
　　　　　But if we scramble
the seasons, bewilder the oak, red or white,
past bearing, will what she knows
change soon enough to fathom another tree,
another nut, and will we?

On Shooting Preserves

Though there are orchids,
                lilies,
                     irises,
                           and asters,
though there are redbuds
              and sweet shrubs,
eight kinds of violet
           and trillium,
                   thrushes,
scarlet tanagers
         and red-tailed hawk,

though the streams teem
             with trout
                  and the forests
with deer,
       in 1910
        George Moore

of Whiting Manufacturing
            wrests
1600 acres from
        the Smoky Mountains

to build for wealthy
          client friends
a shooting preserve

5,000 feet up Hooper's Bald.
              The road wends

rutted, steep.
Twenty-five tons
of double-

strand barbed wire and chestnut rails
to fence
the buffalo and boar,
arriving
in their wooden crates,
bewildered.

A man hired from the U.S. Cavalry

drives the wagon train
toward thinner air.
Eight buffalo,
six Colorado mule deer,
four young wild boar
and fourteen elk.

And just to tease the gentlemen
with fear
six huge Russian browns
among the bears.

Enclosures. Pens. A clubhouse

with two baths.
The wild boar lot stands nine rails
high.

But the winter of 1917
routs autumn like a tusked
snout.

Thirty-five degrees below,
                pipes burst.
It's much too far and cold
                for sporting men.
So the boars root out,
                find feral pigs and mate.

Poachers take the Russian browns,
                the turkeys.
Driven back to Andrews,
                the buffalo are sold.
Elk and mule deer thrive,
                but they're sold too.

Such wily lives that find a way to live,
                thwarted.

At the Turkey Farm

Ghostly sentinels, they stand at the railings,
hundreds deep in the long, dark barn.
Doors opened to the gloaming set free
only the stench of their many pale bodies,
jam-packed, bred featherless and barely winged.
Except a brief sating at feeding,
this is their only solace, to stand
in their own shit, blinking in the fading light.
When we eat them do we take in their longing
for the unentered meadow, their sadness
for the sky they cannot fly into?
Perhaps we become them, soldered to brutal
twilight as their suffered bodies enter our own.
Who will give them back their lives, feathered
and winged? As fair game in the wooded cove,
full of amble and bursts of flight,
their welcomed spirits would not haunt us,
not like these standing naked
pressed against their own deaths.

Strange Meeting

Is this how an animal feels
on the other side of a human eye?

I was a woman speaking
to men I didn't know.

Large and strong, they
knew about power
in ways I may never

I sat framed and assessed
no threat   a square jaw decided
negligible   bent knuckles said

I looked back through my animal
eye, saw

the slit throat of the cow
in the leather shoe

the poisons deep in the soil
where the cotton grew

the felled trees
of the papers stacked

the mountains leveled
in the electric hum of light and heat
where we sat.

I saw clearly

all they had done and would do
to make a world we'd be losing fast.

I saw why it was lost.
And I saw how we would lose it.

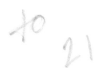

Trackless

After the snow, everything is visible—
sudden hills beyond our familiar ridge
and branches, branches, crazed and woven,
under sleeves of fallen

snow. So I'm climbing the ridge and hoping
tracks of deer or even bear appear, rise up
out of trackless white, some small sign to say
we're here. And not alone.

Father, I am older now than you were, older
now than, dying, you were. The snow ahead
is all unmarked. And friendless, a blank of heavy
cold. Where are they,

bobcat, deer, coyote, the tracks to follow
up this ridge? In deep, then in deeper. Walking
stick and boot. These marks, they're mine, and
leaving them as if leaving

you, again, alone, is what the snow is saying
I'm to do. Ahead, then. The trackless white. But
look. Behind, the snow is riven, riven.
I cannot look. And

turning, climbing, I make such signs
as daughters make, my marks in new snow, however
welcome, hoof and paw of those I can only
love, but not save, not

save. And you? Now overhead, circling, calling,
hawks are parting the air. And if, landing,
their talons mark the branches, the shifted snow
may never reach us here

below. No track, no earthbound sign to lead us on.
Just wings, and the memory of wings. Just cries,
and the memory of cries. After snow
everything not visible.

Part of experience
of working
through this
material —
a quest for
success

uw
p. 9

Sapphic stanzas
— early on
of my father
for whom the
dominant

culture's
scripts didn't
fit, for there
where there
was alternative

to 33

Driving Home

The girl in platform pink flip-flops
stumbles in my headlights on the broken
pavement.
        Beside her, the boy in the gray
overcoat pulls her from the road
in January rain.
        My foot on the brake,
she was never in danger, except perhaps—

her face now contorted by tears—

from the misapprehension
that here in this fractured public space

unmended asphalt
        absence of sidewalks
anonymous, glaring cars

she is somehow to blame.

After the Election, My Mother Rakes Leaves

She tells me she woke before dawn.
Grief burned her right out of her bed.
Her small house in a southern suburb
stirred and blinked in deranged autumn leaves.
She would not live this day like another,
so she took up her rake in the dark.

Common out of all context. Rake in the dark.
Alone, almost eighty, my mother outdoors, dawn
still an hour away. She would not live another
day, not like this one, tilted out of her bed,
faces of the needless dead like leaves
rising up at each stroke in the silent suburb.

How else to live this southern suburb
but to take up a rake in the dark?
This is where the years have brought her, to leaves,
raking leaves in the dark before dawn,
the familiar made strange among dim flowerbeds,
shutter-whiskered windows, every other

house still asleep. Perhaps, now, another
war. How to sleep in the silent suburb
while those others are killed in their beds?
She takes up her rake in the autumn dark
to do clear, certain work before dawn.
Fallen, huddled, now gathered, leaves

lie at the curb. She almost believes
she sees bodies mounded, the other side
of the world, darkening, as dawn
happens here. First light in the suburb
and the houses stand naked, dark
lingering like a bad intention. Misled,

a streetlight illuminates nothing. Beds
of roses need mulching, but she'll leave
that for later. A vote cast in the dark,
she heads in for coffee, another
beginning in the southern suburb.
Her anger rakes down the dawn.

Mulch

When we spread mulch, forking
the fragrant heap to swaddle
roses, their stubbed branches
cut back before bloom,

I open newspapers
to the year I want to forget
and lay down on the bare earth
leaf after leaf of headlines

Taliban Ready for Holy War
Sharon Defies US Pressure
Terrorist Assault
Refugees Rebel

If I thought this a necessary violence,
that the world needs blood poured out
like a fire needs what will burn,
I would gather the winding sheets,
prepare my prayers, shape rituals
for suffering the inevitable.

But I don't.
Death is enough,
takes its portion early or late
without our help.

And it is earth, finally,
what I bend to now
again and again, to tend,
particular ground and what it contains,

we defile by so much defending.

As I lay down the stories of war
and coming war
I want each changed, slowly,
to what will do these plants good:

the absence of weeds,
moisture in drought,
sustenance sufficient for bloom.

After Zazen

Autistic boys in England
                         swallowed stones,
he said, and had to have their stomachs
                                      cut and sewn.
Not pumped? I didn't ask. So heavy,
                         stones.
They must be fetched,
                         even when they've been thrown
down throats that young and small.
                                      You can't blame them.
They want so much to die. And no one asked

anything more. We didn't want
                         to know them,
the boys who made heaviness
                         manifest.
That morning our country
                         had invaded
another country.
                         We felt bereft.

Ashamed. The Buddhist priest finished

his story. We saw how suffering
                         woke
to find itself alive again,
                         famished.

How to Lose a Democracy

someone is lost two steps from home
in waist-high snow
                                        Anna Akhmatova

First, believe you can have
whatever you want
whenever you want it.

Make the desire concrete—
white goods or appliances or jewelry—
anything you can't afford.

And let someone else define it,
so that what you do not need
you cannot do without.

Forget the night sky
and clear water over rocks after rain.
Forget to say what you see,
and courage, forget courage entirely.

Cede what you know to be right
to comfort and plenty. Ask the land
to bear each wound. Ask the animals
to leave their nests and lairs.

Having lost so much, it will be easy
to unhinge language,
to unname each flower and tree.

You see how little it will take

to fail at what you say you believe.

History will say you lost your nerve,
if anyone has the nerve to write history.

Touring the Czech Republic

Taut and lean as good mileage,
our Czech tour guide refuses
each English article, fends off *a*'s
and *the*'s like unwelcome attentions.

Embattled raconteur, she's tired
of the stories on offer
communist liberal conservative
each an unfaithful lover.

The planes of her face
rise to crow's feet, spread
like the fans we wave
in this soaring midsummer heat.

We can barely pronounce the names
of the towns where she takes us,
her raised umbrella the beacon
we follow through a fog of lineage—

Czech noblemen, castles, chateaux.
Stowed in the 11th, the 13th, the 17th
centuries, we're safe, the narrative
taking us to places we know,

mantras of power and wealth
lulling us like the long afternoon.
But the real story happens now.
Fifteen years since the Velvet Revolution

franchises spring up like mushrooms.

The government grants reparations,
old families restored to extravagant wealth.
Havel sells his land for a cool seven million.

Swamped by narrative, without heroes,
we shift in our comfortable seats
listening for a story we haven't heard.
Tonight our Czech tour guide will lead

us to a hotel the Communists built.
Stolid high-rise gutted and remade
for tourists, its windows stand open
like doors on an advent calendar.

Inside, our rooms licked by breeze,
we ask ourselves whether, ten years
from now, others will face the windows
sealed, an air-conditioned staleness

humming *the same, the same, the same.*

2

O somewhere there is a beautiful myth of sorting,
of sifting through a mountain of dross to find the
    one seed.

                                   Paula Meehan

Stroke
for Barb

And suddenly the world shifted.
You were no longer in it.

Before telephones, telegrams.
Before telegrams, messengers on horseback.

There is no way to keep such news back.
It comes during heavy rain

on the heels of a hurricane.
It comes disembodied, your husband's

voice, and you now beyond reach
at least in the ordinary, daily way

of cards and trips and the bright lilt
at the end of the line.

How often did we listen and speak
each other into new lives?

No coincidence, then,
that the day before your death

my own chest constricted with fear,
fear of dying, that old visitor,

so that I woke the morning

you died surprised to be alive.

As if we'd parted on the river's shore
and I'd not crossed with you.

If you were here, I could tell you
this story. Stoic in your disbelief,

but listening, listening me
through it, you'd smile at

that ambling other world
I think I see. You'd say

you're nowhere now
but here's your madcap laugh

from the nuthatch, your tall
sway in the willow, curly hair

in the coral bells.

to p. 53

When the hornets swarmed

                    angry
                             from their nest
(and I write this
                angry
                      that the earth could
open like that
             and suddenly
                         menace and pain)
one hung
          in the air
               like a fury
like a signature
             I'd remember.
                      The others
chose cheek
          and inner thigh
                    (now swell and
throb
        now red hot
               consequence)
until I was all
          howl and jig
                    (but those are not
words for fear—
          they followed me like torment
like a scald
          they left red swathes)
                    and I ran
and swerved
          inside to my books

                              breathless
where I found
                it takes the venom of one hundred
stings
          to die.

To Have You Back

All day I work at borders.
Moss phlox grows through heathers.

Ajuga covers smoky slate.
I untangle the cascading rose

from a volunteer buckeye,
unearth a dandelion's taproot

long as my forearm, but
these boundaries between beds

and bermuda grass won't stay.
Going back to the mountain

the old-timers say as the locusts
sprout, impatient to take back my labor

and love, my squander of time,
my desire for a measurable, momentary beauty.

And you? Back there on your city streets,
what rose up beneath pavement

and foundations, came through concrete,
determined as bramble and bindweed

to have you back? If I stand between
now and then, walk these woods talking

as if I could step one foot over to you,
it's because I'm no longer sure

how to place stone on stone.
If you're there and I'm here,

I want something less certain between us.
Just this wandering hedge of moss rose.

Just the edge of these mapled woods
inviting me in.

Trying to Tell the Truth

All year we lived in the mouth of the lie.

No one could unsay it
though each tried in her way.

This one took her lone breast
out through the keyhole
and never came back.

That one gathered up
her wounded daughter
and flew north.

The rest of us stayed,
knocking at the door of it,
tripping on its coattails,

finally living with it
like an unwelcome neighbor

whose choice to move beside us
we regret

because we're called to friendliness
we do not feel—

wave and barely smile—

until the many greetings,
half-hearted as they are,

confound us to trust
what cannot be trusted.

And here we reach the edge of the known world.

Except This

That she spoke, twice, and he didn't hear her.
Or rather, he put her words in the mouths
of two different men. On record, they said
what she'd said. Not omission. Misattribution.

He put her words in the mouths of two men.
And her own voice was rain in strong wind.
What she'd said. Not omission. Misattribution.
Nonetheless, her voice in that arid room.

For him she was rain in wind.
He was a man like other men.
Her voice, nonetheless, in that arid room—
hitched breath and start, swerve and near miss.

When she sees he's a man like other men,
it's like braking for a rabbit or stray cat:
that hitched breath and start, swerve and near miss.
Small miracle. Not to see what's not there.

It's like braking for a rabbit or stray cat.
She looks back at the now-empty road.
Small miracle, not to see what's not there.
Nothing wounded but her already wounded heart.

She looks back at the empty road.
For the record, these are her words and voice.
Nothing wounded but her wounded heart.
That she spoke, twice, and he didn't hear.

Recalling Virginia Woolf

After his thirteenth confident
pronouncement
on music, poetry, politics,
I'm Lily Briscoe once more
afraid when I look again
I won't see what I see.

He's shifted a poet I love
right off the canvas.
She's flecks of paint on my shoes.
She's nice, alright, but
as if he's Adam naming
the animals and I myself
am new to the world,
just invented, bonehead
pulled from his side.

I won't beat him at this—
that's certain—his own head
more full of facts and opinions
than cellars millennialists stock
with provisions for the end of the world.

Anger stokes me all morning.
I'm the moth with the ragged wing
batting the glass pane.
Outside in the open air
swallows light on the eaves
shaking their forked tails.

Dog Dreams

Ceilidh's muzzle is burning.

She is not an angry dog,

but in the dream she is angry.

I construct her as angry.

Amiable dog, she will do this for me,

be my symbol.

She lies on her side, resting,

pale plume of fire at her mouth,

dark eyes waiting.

Then the scene shifts

and I shout at a man who loves power.

I know who you are, I snarl,

but he waves me away.

A bitch with her teeth bared

is a serious warning.

The jowls of the man twitch.

He's more than half fear.

Ceilidh settles on her haunches.

She will not pierce his thigh with her two fangs.

She will not crush his hand with her powerful jaws.

Believe me. She will not tear out his throat.

The Zen Master Yells

at me.
　　　　The gong has rung
　　　　　　　　　　its deep-throated
command, and I have not stopped
　　　　　　　　　　　　raking leaves
toward the absence of human speech.
　　　　　　　　　　　　　Dogged,
I intend to finish this task,
　　　　　　　　only
that's not the point,
　　　　　　　later he will tell me,
another Westerner
　　　　　　stubborn as flint.

He glares from under the dripping eaves
at me in the drizzle
　　　　　　　among yellow prints
of mostly maple,
　　　　　　breaks the silence
where all morning
　　　　　　I've sat
　　　　　　　　in my woman's
body. *Sesshin. Zazen.*
　　　　　　Joints flaring,
　　　　　　　　　　resistant,
I don't give up my ego
　　　　　　like a man.

Removing Moles

She is all precision, the needle held
low, beyond my field of vision, the scalpel—
I never see it do its work. Ample
Novocain. I don't feel a thing but old,
old enough to indulge this fear of death
as she stitches me up. *Dysplastic nevus,*
treated by surgery and surveillance.
Struck by sun, ozone loosening like gauze,
my body's been unruly enough
to admit a potential for dying.
But that secret must be kept as a gaze
is kept from those too beautiful, or grieving.
Stanched for now the inevitable raze
of what we build between ourselves and leaving.

Well Before Danger
for Karen

Surprised by your summer funeral
we drift in
                    in our improvised mourning

called inland from Edisto, Myrtle Beach,
fishing rods laid down at Manteo,

we come in our sandals
and discount-house blacks
bought beside the highway.

We don't wear these clothes
as if we believed in them.

Instead, we are all of us wishing
the bullet back in the gun,
the gun in its unopened drawer,
even back on the store shelf.

Easy enough to get rid of the weapon,
but what's left is your lover's anger,
so deadly we're here
beside the closed casket.
We're stuck at the end of a story
his own temple entered
like yours

and we don't know how to walk
that narrative back—
we don't know
where to find you

well before danger, beloved,

both bullets back in a gun
that has never been forged.

Millennium ii

Pinned between trees
> in a ravine
my old dog is learning
> something new.

Near midnight, the moon's
> opaque face
nearly round, he howls
> across all his twelve years.

He is late coming to this much
> wildness,
domestication
> a well worn collar,
> > training
bone deep. But tonight
> seizures shed it all
like an undercoat.
> Misfiring, but hardly
misled,
> he's quarrelling with duality,

ready to join the coyote on the ridge

whose tide of raspy scat calls

make no bones about it.
> And who am I
with my untethered lead,
> edging down

the slippery slope, but a species

out of its mind

being out of its body, come this eleventh hour

to retrieve what I love

gone strange.

Stubbornly Green
for Susan

Driving back to my blue mountains,
I am less than ever at home.
Another bomb blast in Iraq—
46 dead, 90 wounded—refuses
to recede to background noise.
I turn the radio off.

When I was younger, the future
was all pulse and promise,
but middle age doesn't offer
many bluffs.
        I suppose I believed
in something like progress, ascent,
however gradual, like this ribbon of road
from Lenoir to Blowing Rock,
the way I hardly notice I've risen
from the piedmont hills
until sheer rock face on the right side
and a sharp drop to streams on the left
reminds me.
        It's we humans
who love the straight line, want
to be spared the looped intercessions
of mourning and grief, even though
all around us—the whorl of seasons,
day and night at each others heels.

I'm not retreating to theories of inevitable war,
but I know the dead have to be mourned.

If we're going anywhere at all
surely it's nowhere we know,
the route more like a good conversation,
all give and take, not the hard drive
of the rock-and-roll beat
our soldiers play during battle.

Now even this road I'm on winds,
an engineer deciding years ago, I suppose,
not to blast through solid rock.
I wend past rhododendron and mountain laurel,
stubbornly green through each long winter.
Spring takes its time here—
we'll be weeks behind your azaleas.
Like my saying what you already know,
I've grown accustomed to late blooming.

News from Midlife

raw, you are silk before
it is spun, the unyolked egg

watch without a wrist

not the tree, but anticipation
of the tree nestled in the nut

unmended boot, unripe papaya,
unbought trousers

yes, you are all those
upended expectations

the bell before the clapper collides
with what it takes for the other side

empty flue above
                          the unbuilt fire
untied shoe

oh you
undo, undo, undo

Natal Chart

Like a bad break on a pool table
where balls stay bunched,
none sinking easily into a pocket,

my planets land opposed,
Venus staring down Mars,
Mars scowling at Neptune.

It's enough to send me
into the arms of Yeats
after his Steinach treatments.
Or back to the garden
to sit naked with Blake,
waiting for the next vision.
Both believed the odd clash,
the smack of will on will,
necessary for the new.

What else to do but fall
in love with the cosmic
arm wrestle, tango
with a shadow,
let the sparks fly
up my flue?

If we're hitched to the tides
by our own watery bodies,
perhaps the planets do
pick us up by the scruff,
set us down in the den of our lives.

Venus at daggers with Uranus,
I catch the heat from each blow,
careful the commotion
doesn't send me up,
more fight than flame.

Oblique

Years ago I had you
on the tip of my tongue—

we were that close
to a dangerous language.

You were such a disarming
lover of vowels,

I couldn't believe
a word you said.

Then you took up
spelling backwards

and I refused
to rhyme.

We turned ornery dictions
in a room where someone else slept.

These days we aren't
in the same dictionary.

I wonder what will become
of us, you once said

as if you might be
someone else.

And you are.
O tundra lips,
O caged and virulent heart.

In Blood Only

People who do not secrete their blood type antigens in other fluids besides blood are called, reasonably enough, non-secretors ....There is some evidence that the non-secretor is genetically older...and may have been more compatible with the digestive needs of hunter-gatherers. Peter D'Adamo

They show up in detective novels
as the ones who can be found
because of what cannot be found,
their mucus with no trace of O or A or B.
They carry that information
in blood only.

Like the first woman and man,
their bodies are ancient,
even when young,
and they have the second sight.

Their hearts are undefended.
They remember time like trees.
They may be tempted to turn
against their own tissue—
because the boundary of I and *other*
is blurred, they embrace perfect strangers.

Sometimes they ask themselves
why they are here, among so many
human refinements. Like alligators,
they are still but quick
at the right moment.

Her Hatred

Her lip curled. I could see
that she hated me.
                    It was odd

how the hatred went on
for days and days and years and years.

I began to feel I could
count on it. It was a steady

reliable hatred. Not like
baled hay
            which can rot.

Or a hollyhock
                    which a woodchuck
can whittle to twig.

Her hatred was solid and determined
like petrified wood.

And though it needed no tending,
she tended it.
                    For instance,
she never spoke to me,
for fear, perhaps, I would damage the hatred

soil its purity, its utter rightness.
But certainly she spoke of me

to others, to shine up the hatred,
to make it glow.

So that finally I felt
her hatred was her gift

and when she offered it up,
I thanked her, silently,

for the strange vigil she kept with it,
knowing at last she had nothing else.

Mysterious Friendship

Silences between women
are overgrown flowerbeds.

Even the daylilies, left unattended,
yield to bermuda grass.

Mid-August and I'm weary of weeding
though I do weed, grudgingly,

careful not to wake
the small spokes of pain

that wheel toward my back
if I'm careless.

Coral bells choke in the crab grass.
Heathers pout beneath pokeweed.

What I tried to say
you preferred unsaid,

so here's the ragweed
between us, the beggar ticks

and bitter cress, the cleavers and nettle.
In this wilderness, nightshade's as likely

as Queen Anne's lace, brambles
and cockleburs as multiflora rose,

though once I found a wild orchid

in the burdock and goutweed

at the edge of the woods.
When I gave it air and light,

exposed the ethereal stalk,
the single striped tongue,

it shrank back, all my care
unwelcome, willing to thrive

only when hidden,
surrounded by weeds.

Some Rough Justice

That way of being a woman—
strappy heels, Chanel no. 5 at her wrist—
there was something about it
she no longer recognized.

A perfectly balanced imbalance?
She wasn't sure, but even though
she was way beyond teetering,
had mastered the angle years ago
so that the scent of sex
followed each step she took,

she was more than half sure
she wanted her heels on the ground,
her body fragrant with essential oils,
rose, citrus, lavender.

I won't say a lover's tryst failed,
she hung her high-heeled sandals beside
the ramshackle barn and never
went back. That isn't what happened,

though she might have taken off her clothes
at dusk, sandals last, and entered the open
meadow, quite alone.

Whatever it was, some rough justice
brought her down to earth

not to the absence of love
as she'd feared

but to give and take
quiet as a whisper
the ear tries not to hear.

Meteor Dream

Though I looked over my shoulder
like someone asked to dance
who cannot image herself
anyone's choice,
                it chose me.
First a shower far away,
then a persistent throb of light.

Animated matter, intent,
it singled me out, then made itself
small and benevolent, a glowing

handful, that smacked my window
as I watched, and iridescent,
formerly molten, now warm,

slid malleable into someone's hands
as others gathered around.

I don't know if they knew it was mine.
But I knew.

3

What is this joy? That no animal
falters, but knows what it must do?

Denise Levertov

Canning Globalization

Not raised during the Depression
I get it wrong.
Canning's not a thing you do
for fun or novelty.

It's what might go
to waste out in the yard.
Figs and pears and muscadines.
Blueberries from a cousin's laden bushes.

It's readiness at the brimming,
a steadfast looking out
for what's been given.

Mother, I want to learn this gathering,
this shoring up against eventualities.

Earthquake. Mudslide. Hurricane.
Buried and drowned wait at the doors
of our dreams. Shall we meet them
improvident, all our shelves empty?

Mother, teach me the boiling,
the cooling and sealing,
how to live on these two acres,
squash vines on the upper hill,
raspberries in the sloping meadow.

*Because those trapped in the rubble
were not dug out in time.*

Because others waited for days
on a bridge without water.

I take tongs to the boiled jars
and fill them with pears you bring me
from the tree my father planted
thirty years ago.

From his hands to yours to mine.

We are building a house
that will stand on moving earth,
levees to hold the waters' rising.
We are leaving our cars beside the road
so drought will not kill the crops.

Mother, teach me to let the jars stand and cool.
Let me peaceably fill my shelves
and bring on no one's calamity.

1957

I was six months old, and you took me
from a South you'd never left,
both of us new to this,
how airplanes and taxis could lift
poor girls out of the sticks.

Now I'd never be from there.
Father had made the arrangements,
left you with *yes* or *no*.
You said you never looked back,
launched me into the world
as soon as I caught breath,
to San Francisco and the boat
that took us across the Pacific
where you stood in the cabin's
threshold, a farm girl on an ocean liner,
and saw you were to do
something else you'd never done,
share time and space
with a woman whose skin was black.

I'd stay with her girls while she went
to the movies. Then she'd watch you
and I'd go. We'd all eat dinner together
and play bingo.

You tell me this now
when each of our sins
and omissions
has left us with nothing
but a new start.

And here it is
fear rising in your belly
as you stand in a doorway.

While Dr. King was dreaming
his dream and Rosa sat where she liked,
a white girl left the Jim Crow south,
became a citizen of the mottled world
and took me.

to
94

The Floor

The carpet came up
                    in wide soggy strips,

the waffled backing dense
                    with moisture,
a spongy mess
                    we could hardly handle.

It came up like the past
                    with sticking points

that stubbornly adhere
                    and won't give way.

And it was something far more
                    comprehensive
anyway that we intended

by lifting carpet from concrete.

We worked without the safety
                    of wood, of tile, of stone

knowing we'd find nothing lovely there
                    to recover,
no neglected oak or hidden slate

no labor done before our time
                    and left for us
                    to restore.
But we were denied
                    even the bald face of concrete.

Instead, a sticky latex

                blotched the surface

what we'd been standing on

                    botched too,

by the misapplied, the unexamined,

                        the often

unintended.

But what to stand on

                while clearing

                      a place to stand?

Old socks

            that browned and tracked

as we pushed wet mops

                and plunged them into

murky buckets.

We felt half-mad

            at 2 a.m.

                    sopping the endless floor

ungrounded

            the ugly layers coming up

like a bad narrative.

But there was no

            turning back.

Between the floor we'd had,

                  an abject certainty
of stains and mold,
          and the stark promise

of what we hoped to make,

the concrete slab emerged,
                indecorous
but solid
      enough to bear
             whatever weight,
whatever change.

And yet, amorphous as origins—

stone and sand, gravel, pebbles and cement,

some miracle of mixing and of parts

like being and the ground of being.

In the face
       of that vast level

we backed off
        from the absolute,
playfully,
       provisionally,

laid down an eggshell white

and with acrylic blues
         simulated smoky tile,
the thing itself

we suspected
         far more than we could afford,

the thing itself
      we decided
            not what we were after.

Gone in Water

By one detail I am comforted—

that you left this world
                    as you'd arrived,
naked,
        washed clean,

gone in a ritual of water
                    beneath the showerhead,
swift, wet slide
                to the other side,
no lingering,
            no dipping in a toe,

but a decisive shift

beyond breath,
                beyond memory,
beyond reason.

Gone to water
                the Cherokee say.
Gone in water.

And who among us thinks

we'd wish to leave quietly

in our sleep?

Changing Forecast

All morning I am weather.
Lashing rain clearing to sun.
Then rain. Then sun. Then rain.

That elm outside my window
is bearing it, limbs tossed
in every direction, tousled crown.

I am bearing it too—
now elm, surely anchored,
now wind, aimless bluster—

one wild rooted dance.

Before and After
for Pat and Quail

Before the present grandeur of your cathedral-
ceilinged kitchen, its stained glass poised for first

light, before colanders swaddled pasta there
or centerpieces shown with amethyst and pearl,

the same hum of language and laughter
filled a smaller space of countertops crowded

with cookbooks and pots, plates of spring rolls,
Chinese dumplings, bowls of steaming rice,

the same fierce stove shouted its syllables
of heat as two Dalmatians laid their anvil heads

side by side, and the same passion pealed past
bedposts out into the land, the thirty acres bought

in pieces over twenty years where horses arrived
to graze, their long necks sloping toward

meadow grass and blueberry bushes took root,
blossomed and dreamed their fruit,

where the spikes of irises finally unfurled toward
the plenty of bluegrass and babies, books and

ballads, mandolins, trombones and bass, Volvos
and snub-nosed pickups, motorcycles and Morgans,

silences and shouting, beer and cigarettes,
Baptists and Lutherans, highways and backroads,

high school, grad school, art school,
precinct and parish, pottery and sculpture,

which is, after all, what labor and the heart
can make of many years.

Ars Poetica

*Choose a subject that is suited to your abilities, you who aspire
to be writers; give long thought to what you are capable of
undertaking, and what is beyond you.*   Horace

I considered writing a poem
      in praise of the A-line skirt

but my heart wasn't in it.

Sure, I wanted to celebrate
      elegant simplicity
           flat seams and flair without flounce,

but sixteen children are dead in Beirut
because they lived near a Hezbollah target.

They are matted hair and blood
sometimes in so many pieces
they cannot be reassembled for graves

and I live in the country
that made the weapons
that killed them.

So my moment of praise and play
      doesn't open like a lily
           doesn't fill the room with fragrance.

If beauty is truth and truth beauty,
who sewed these seams for pennies,
sat with the vat of toxic dyes,
drank the runoff water

with the cotton's pesticides

who lost his child,
who lost her life

while I sit in my A-line skirt,
suddenly ashes and shroud?

On Being Told Not to Use the Word
Moral

I'll admit it's rusty with disuse
so when I say it lately in a group,

it comes up like machinery through sludge.
I might as well have said *you stupid butt*

or pulled a ruler out to measure skirts
an inch above the knee as said that word,

moral. It's lost to us, most certainly,
as absolutes on tablets from Yahweh,

and I'm okay with that, except for this:
we'll never leave behind thou shalt not kill,

and why can't we decide that genocide
is not a thing that human beings do?

If moral codes were like old recipes,
some we'd honor and not change, because we

found them good. Others we'd adapt because
ingredients grow scarce. Some we'd put away

entirely. So if morality's
an open-ended, provisional tease,

ineffectual unless contextual,
why ever mess around with absolutes?

And yet I find I want to say just this:
Let every human being be nourished

by shelter, food, and care so that all gifts
flourish. And let us love the animals.

And let us love the land. Now that's a code,
forgive me, I'd certainly call *moral*.

Saying No to Thunder

Herding dogs, they rush out
as if sound could be corralled.

First up the wooded west trail,
then south down the sloping meadow,
they bark the thunder back.

When lightning puts its cloven hoof
to the ground, they are always
at the heel of it. Their fur sodden,
they run, relentless as pelting rain,
toward what they have done with fear.

They would burst their hearts for this,
the belief in their blood and bones,
that this labor is theirs alone.

They charge each clap and rumble
until the work is done.

Rescuing the Garden

Like the tender center of celery,
a calla lily sends up one pale yellow arm.

I've papered and laid down mulch
thinking I'd outsmart weeds.

But here's proof that we keep out
more than we know with all our protection.

So I dig for the lost ones
and find their thick stalks
tunneling into the dark.

What did it take for that arm
to break free, signal to the others?

Once above ground, they cower,
naked and stunned by release.

Fetal, unearthly. I wish them green.
I have found them in time.
I am sure of it.

Kundalini,

the coil at the base
of being, the tailbone
unsprung, my body
singing desire as if
it's the only song
I know. This spring
morning, I count the years
I might have left
for that feral, pelty self
I found in her forties,
bare-breasted, open-mouthed,
all risk and moan.

She woke to the aching alarm,
to the odometer throbbing,
to the tape measure thrusting its tongue.

She woke to the fine print,
to the belching calendar,
to the regime of the dotted line.

She woke to the staggering hours
before deadline. Then the herald
arrives: *This is your life and no other.*

I was all patience and planning and tact.
But she woke with demands, manifestos.
So clawing and bawling, I turn to you,
and make love like there's no tomorrow.

Our Held Animal Breath

Here at the conference hotel
I keep one foot in another world.

Forget what city I'm in—
each room is a piece of unripe fruit

shipped from a factory farm.
We school in fluorescent twilight

try to be wise without windows,
open ourselves in the unopened air.

Smitten with sameness, we're lost together,
collecting sore throats and coughs

so outside when we gather on concrete
across from the parking garage

we gasp when the rabbit appears
alone on the exit ramp

and wait to see how on earth
it lives here, between wheels and exhaust,

as if watching whatever is left
of our warm and vulnerable selves.

A leap at the last moment
into the managed green

of a flowerbed, all uniform,
unopened bulbs and we cheer

because, for the moment, escape,
survival in the common release

of our held animal breath.

CPSIA information can be obtained at www.ICGtesting.com
Printed in the USA
LVOW051537170912

299161LV00004B/162/P